Growing Your Prayer Life

Six Principles to Plant Deeper Roots and Bear Greater Fruit

Dale Roach

Copyright © 2018 by **Dale Roach**

All rights reserved. No part of this publication may be reproduced, distributed, or transmitted in any form or by any means, without prior written permission.

Scripture quotations marked (NASB) are taken from the New American Standard Bible ® (NASB), copyright © 1960, 1962, 1963, 1968, 1971, 1972, 1973, 1975, 1977, 1995 by The Lockman Foundation. Used by permission. www.Lockman.org.

Scripture quotations marked (NIV) are taken from the Holy Bible, New International Version. Copyright © 1973, 1978, 1984, 2011 by Biblica, Inc.® Used by permission. All rights reserved worldwide.

Sermon To Book
www.sermontobook.com

Growing Your Prayer Life / Dale Roach
ISBN-13: 978-1-945793-33-2
ISBN-10: 1-945793-33-3

This book is dedicated to the people in my life who have taught we many lessons about talking with God. To all those saints who have gone home to be with their Lord. There was a little boy, named Dale, sitting in the church pew, who listened to how you prayed. Thank you!

CONTENTS

Made for Prayer 3

Hallowed Be Thy Name: The Prayer Principle of Worshiping God 13

Thy Kingdom Come: The Prayer Principle of Bringing God's Kingdom to the Earth 27

Give Us This Day: The Prayer Principle of Trusting in God's Provision 41

Forgive Us Our Trespasses: The Prayer Principle of Seeking God's Forgiveness 53

Lead Us Not into Temptation: The Prayer Principle of Relying on God's Protection 65

Thine Is the Kingdom, the Power, and the Glory: The Prayer Principle of Showcasing God's Kingdom, Power, and Glory 79

Notes 93

About the Author 96

About Sermon To Book 98

INTRODUCTION

Made for Prayer

If we are honest, each of us has a deep-seated desire in our inner hearts to be able to talk with God—to really commune with Him. We want to know what He says about our lives and to have our deepest needs, longings, and desires heard by our Creator. The preacher and theologian Charles Spurgeon once said that all of us at some point in our lives will have the need or the desire to pray. He wrote:

> I believe that man prays because there is something in prayer. When the Creator gives ... the power of thirst, it is because water exists to meet its thirst. When He creates hunger, there is food to correspond to the appetite. Even so, when He inclines men to pray, it is because prayer has a corresponding blessing connected with it.[1]

At some point in our lives, we all will have this strong desire to talk with God. But whether or not we choose to do so is completely in our control.

Humans have possessed this overwhelming need to talk with God—to speak to Him and to hear His response—since the beginning of creation. This longing to talk with the heavenly Father was a yearning that one of the twelve disciples expressed to Jesus after His interactions with the Father had been observed for some time:

> *One day Jesus was praying in a certain place. When he finished, one of his disciples said to him, "Lord, teach us to pray, just as John taught his disciples.* — **Luke 11:1 (NIV)**

Some people have said that prayer is to religion what research is to science.[2] In other words, it is an attempt to foster a personal relationship with our Creator that goes beyond what we presently know or experience. Prayer is an action that is solely focused on building a relationship with God. In fact, prayer and the word *relationship* cannot be separated from one another.

My Early Experience with Prayer

One of the greatest blessings that the Lord gave me when I was a child was to grow up in a Christian home. Personal conversations were an active part of my early life as a child, both among our family members and between my family members and God through prayer. I often heard my parents speaking to one another with an attitude of affection and respect, and they talked to me and my brother and sister in the same manner.

These interactions that I recall from my childhood took place not only among the people in my family, but also with the heavenly Father, His Son, and the Holy Spirit. This dialogue included everything from where we should live and what we should do to the smallest details of our lives. I have vivid memories of my parents talking to God on a regular basis.

I am convinced that the reason I am a happy, practicing Christian today is because of this early introduction to the healthy communication between my family members. Talking to God has always been a natural part of my life. Early on, my parents convinced me that God *wants* to communicate with me about my life, and there has never been any reason for me to doubt that lesson.

This experience of talking to God extended from my childhood circle into another family as I grew older. When I met my wife and was introduced to her parents, I quickly realized that they also loved one another, they loved their children, and they loved God. The way they talked to one another and with the Lord revealed to me once again that He desires to communicate with us.

When I was a young child, I spent one summer with my grandparents in Chesnee, South Carolina, while my father was attending seminary in New Orleans. In all the years that have passed since that time, those Sundays when I attended a small Wesleyan church outside of Spartanburg that my grandfather pastored remain ingrained in my mind.

One woman who made a deep impression on me at that very church always sat on the second pew to the right of my grandfather as he stood in the pulpit. Her dress was always a dark color, and her hair was snow white and always rolled up into a bun. I remember both her appearance and the conversations we shared as pleasant and kind.

However, the times when my grandfather called on her to pray made the strongest mark on my young mind. When this saintly woman would begin her prayer, I assumed—quite correctly—that she knew the One to whom she was talking because the conversation was so personal and so intimate between the two of them. During her prayers, she spoke as if she had the utmost respect for the One with whom she was engaging in prayer. There was no stammering, no lack of words, and even more unusual in many Christian circles, no use of unusual phrases and Bible lingo, or "Christianese." Instead, she talked directly to the God who created her and who knew every detail of her life.

I can remember being impressed as a child by her obviously deep and personal relationship with God. This must have been how the disciples felt when they heard Jesus praying to His Father. It was obvious there was something personal going on.

Something's Missing

I must confess that even though I have been surrounded by those who talk with God, the actual act of prayer has always been a challenge for me. Although I have known that God is present in my life and that He desires to communicate His thoughts and plans with me and hear my needs, fears, hopes, and dreams in return, the world in which I live has developed an extreme counterculture that works against healthy conversations of all kinds. We struggle to talk with human beings as well as with our Creator in prayer.

In my opinion, many of our modern resources, such as text messaging or new apps like Snapchat and Instagram available on our electronic devices, have eroded the quality of our face-to-face communication skills with other human beings—and with God. We miss out on the slow, deepening relationship-building that develops through long, intimate conversations over a dinner table with each other, or in prayer with our heavenly Father.

Our modern ways of communication are nothing at all like Jesus' when He took His disciples away from the business of the day and off to a quiet place to pray (see Mark 6:31). But Jesus' methods are vitally important, because prayer is all about personal communication with God. And this type of deep and intimate communication calls for followers of Christ to commit to listening as much as talking when they spend time with God.

I have written this particular book on prayer because of the "conversational prayer life" that was introduced to me long ago in my childhood by the people who loved me the most. Their ability to communicate with the living Lord opened my heart as a little boy to understand how important it was to talk with Him and to hear from Him on a regular basis about things that mattered to my life.

Paul E. Miller writes that finding God and being able to communicate with Him require us to be childlike. Jesus told His disciples to ask like a child and to believe like a child. This process of praying will open up our hearts to trust God in the same way that a young child trusts his parents (see Matthew 7:9–11). Miller simplifies this way of living by writing, "To learn how to pray is to enter the world of a child, where all things are possible."[3]

My eyes were opened when that precious elderly woman in my grandfather's church prayed. The idea of *not* watching her pray was more than a child could stand. As she prayed, she allowed my young heart to catch a glimpse of the bond she had with Jesus. Her communication and connection with her Lord and Savior would always conclude with one vivid and dramatic line: "And so, Father, I want to thank You once again, that I have been saved, sanctified, and washed in the blood of the Lamb."

That was a very articulate closing to a prayer, so much so that I have remembered those exact lines, word for word, into my adult years.

The prayers of Christians in my life have proven to me that real praying is not self-centered, but is fueled by a desire to see God's kingdom take control. However, prayer often can become self-focused. Nothing will expose our selfishness and spiritual weaknesses quicker than honest, heartfelt prayer.

Jesus said:

> *So do not worry, saying, "What shall we eat?" or "What shall we drink?" or "What shall we wear?" For the pagans run after all these things, and your heavenly Father knows that you need them. But seek first His kingdom and his*

righteousness, and all these things will be given to you as well. —Matthew 6:31–33 (NIV)

The foundation of a true prayer life is that of *developing* a relationship with God and building daily upon His plan and His design—not our own personal agendas.

Can We Really Talk to God?

Is it really possible to learn to listen to and communicate with God?

Jesus expected His disciples to talk with their heavenly Father. And when He answered His disciple's question about how to pray, He laid out a clear strategy. Developing an effective prayer life is a process of building the Kingdom.

There are six basic principles that Jesus set forth in the prayer that He taught His disciples to pray, what we call the "Lord's Prayer." Throughout the next six chapters, we will take an in-depth look at Jesus' teaching on each of these principles and see that a strong prayer life is a process that builds upon itself, piece by piece. These are the six foundations for action:

1. The Prayer Principle of Worshiping God
2. The Prayer Principle of Bringing God's Kingdom to the Earth
3. The Prayer Principle of Trusting in God's Provision
4. The Prayer Principle of Seeking God's Forgiveness

5. The Prayer Principle of Relying on God's Protection
6. The Prayer Principle of Showcasing God's Power and Glory

Following these six principles to develop your prayer life can create a clear and open line of communication with the Father of heaven. It will end the chaos and conflict in our personal lives, our relationships, our occupations, and our places of worship, and instead bring a sense of joy, hope, and peace. The disciplined practice of prayer is a solid foundation for your life.

Charles Spurgeon has encouraging words for even those newest to prayer:

> ...prayer itself is an art that only the Holy Spirit can teach us. He is the giver of all prayer. Pray until you can pray. Pray to be helped to pray, and do not give up praying because you cannot pray. It is when you think you cannot pray that you are most praying.[4]

As you read this book, you'll notice that a set of reflective questions and an application-oriented action step accompany each main chapter. I encourage you to engage fully and honestly with these questions and action steps to help you along your journey toward a deeper, more prayerful relationship with God.

And throughout this journey, I encourage you to examine your prayer life and ask yourself one simple question: *Am I following the leadership of Jesus when it comes to developing a relationship with my heavenly Father?*

CHAPTER ONE

Hallowed Be Thy Name: The Prayer Principle of Worshiping God

Our Father in heaven, hallowed be your name...
—Matthew 6:9 (NIV)

If Jesus, God's very Son, the sinless, spotless One, began His own prayer to the Father with a declaration of praise and worship, how much more should you and I do the same? *Worship* is the foundation to all of the other growth that we will experience through a healthy and flourishing prayer life. It is the basis from which all the rest of our prayer will flow. Let's start by saying, with the Master Teacher on prayer: "Hallowed be Thy name!"

Worship in Every Language

Throughout my life, I have experienced a variety of worship styles in a variety of settings, ranging from a Pentecostal Holiness Church in the mountains of North Carolina and a Roman Catholic church in New Orleans to a Russian Orthodox church in Moscow and a village chapel in Bolivia, just to name a few.

My personal spiritual journey has allowed me to see how people praise God in all sorts of different ways. The worship of God is a beautiful experience, no matter what country it is practiced in or in which language it is spoken.

While on the mission trip to Bolivia, I experienced the singing of a hymn in the village church service, in which the only part I actually understood was the sound of the music being played. But even though the words were not being sung in my native tongue, my missionary friends and I were able to sing right along in English and praise God collectively with our Bolivian brothers and sisters. *Real* worship of God was taking place—in two completely different languages at the same time!

When believers gather together and participate in the true worship of their heavenly Father, the results can be powerful. But this is even truer when that kind of true, faultless, uninhibited worship accompanies our prayers.

True Worship Creates the Foundation of Prayer

Beginning our prayers with the worship of God will empower our spiritual growth. It puts us into the right frame of mind and spirit to converse with our Creator. In his book *Prayer: More Than Words*, Leroy Eims tells us what happens in a Christian's life when he or she acknowledges God as "hallowed" and "holy":

> A true vision of God's exalted greatness cannot help but produce feelings of profound humility in us. I cannot stand in the presence of the Lord without being painfully conscious of my own insignificance. The other side of exalting the Lord is humbling myself.[5]

Worship of God must be the foundation of prayer for every believer whose prayers are to flourish and produce good results. But when we speak of worship, what do we really mean? How do we know a true and authentic experience of worship is taking place? How important is it to set aside all of our personal goals, plans, and agendas for just a few moments of time in order to honor God?

The Bible teaches about what true praise and worship means, from the Psalms in the Old Testament through the book of Revelation in the New Testament. Let's take a look at what the Scriptures have to tell us about worship and the benefits it can bring to our life of prayer:

All the earth will worship You, and will sing praises to You; they will sing praises to Your name. — **Psalm 66:4 (NASB)**

Worship the Lord in holy attire; tremble before Him, all the earth. — **Psalm 96:9 (NASB)**

Exalt the Lord our God and worship at His footstool; Holy is He. — **Psalm 99:5 (NIV)**

Praise the Lord in song, for He has done excellent things; let this be known throughout the earth. — **Isaiah 12:5 (NASB)**

Jesus answered him, "It is written, 'You shall worship the Lord your God and serve Him only.'" — **Luke 4:8 (NASB)**

But an hour is coming, and now is, when the true worshipers will worship the Father in spirit and truth; for such people the Father seeks to be His worshipers. God is spirit, and those who worship Him must worship in spirit and truth. — **John 4:23–24** *(NASB)*

Through Him then, let us continually offer up a sacrifice of praise to God, that is, the fruit of lips that give thanks to His name. — **Hebrews 13:15 (NASB)**

...and he said with a loud voice, "Fear God, and give Him glory, because the hour of His judgment has come; worship

*Him who made the heaven and the earth and sea and springs of waters." — **Revelation 14:7 (NASB)***

Charles Colson once wrote that in most churches, "members never really get a sense of worship. When the whole service is geared to an altar call—when that becomes the emotional high point, and when the pressure is put on and the invitation hymn is played endlessly—the purpose of the worship service can be distorted."[6]

Authentic worship can only take place when the *Lord* is the audience, not the worshipers. Real worship is about placing God in His much-deserved position of honor. It is about recognizing how blessed we are, as sinful people, even to be allowed in the presence of God, the Creator of heaven and earth, the Most Holy One in the universe.

When Jesus taught His disciples how to pray, He indicated that, when they called on the name of God, it was to always be done with an attitude of worship and respect. We are always to approach Him in a way that honors His majestic power and strength. We must humbly give thanks by acknowledging His grace and love for His people. Before we ask any favor of God, we are to take the humble position of gratitude and thanks and exalt Him for who He is in our lives. We must always come to Him "in everything by prayer and supplication with thanksgiving…" (Philippians 4:6).

A Hallowed Name

"Hallowed be Thy name"—that's the phrase Jesus used at the beginning of His instructional prayer to show His followers how they should address their heavenly Father. He told them that they should honor God's *name* in their prayers. The word *hallowed* here implies that God is to be greatly revered and respected. In this way of thinking, our prayers must begin by first acknowledging how much we honor God.

Part of calling the Father "hallowed," of honoring Him, involves an attitude of respect. Respect is a behavior that has disappeared in many circles of our world today. When I was a child growing up in the Southern United States, my parents drilled this concept into me in my toddler years: I was to always address my elders with the title "ma'am" or "sir." With that as a starting point, respect for my elders and for those in authority grew naturally, and it has served me well over the years.

In the same way, our prayers to our heavenly Father should first begin with this simple acknowledgment of the respect we have for God. Addressing God in this way is a deliberate action of respect and worship.

Jesus used the term *Abba* when He addressed the Father. This title was a familiar one, a term of endearment frequently used by children. Its closest translation in modern-day English is actually "Daddy." When my kids were young, I can remember them coming up to me and calling me by this name. The term expressed their love, appreciation, and respect for me as their biological father, but also as the one they knew would meet their needs, protect them, and love them unconditionally. And they were respecting me by using it—"hallowing" me, in other words.

When we approach God in prayer, we, too, must honor Him in our words, with what we say, but also in our hearts, in our attitude and posture toward Him, by acknowledging Him as "Daddy"—as the One who loves us unconditionally and meets our needs. We must also demonstrate a level of respect that sets Him aside as holy, sacred, and honored. Our true affections for God will be evident in what we call Him and in how we choose to relate to Him. This particular term of endearment, *Abba*, shows that God is personal in our lives. That was Jesus' intention in demonstrating its use to His followers.

Throughout the Old Testament, God's people had learned to acknowledge Him by many different names, each one meeting a different need or introducing a different aspect of God's character into their psyche. The Jewish people referred to God, their Father, as:

- Elohim: the LORD God: "The earth was formless and void, and darkness was over the surface of the deep, and the Spirit of God [*Elohim*] was hovering over the waters" (Genesis 1:1–2 NIV).

- Jehovah: Lord, master, relational God: "This is the account of the heavens and the earth when they were created, when the LORD [*Jehovah*] God made earth and heavens" (Genesis 2:4 NIV).

- Adonai: Master over all: "O Lord God [*Adonai*] You have begun to show Your servant Your greatness and Your strong hand; for what god is there in heaven or on earth who can do such works and mighty acts as Yours?" (Deuteronomy 3:24 NASB).

- El Shaddai: Almighty God: "When Abram was ninety-nine years old, the Lord appeared to him and said, 'I am God Almighty [*El Shaddai*]; walk before me faithfully and be blameless. Then I will make my covenant between me and you and will greatly increase your numbers'" (Genesis 17:1–2 NIV).

- Immanuel: God with us: "Therefore the Lord Himself will give you a sign: Behold, a virgin will be with child and bear a son, and she will call His name *Immanuel*" (Isaiah 7:14 NASB).

Worship Is Inevitable!

In the account of his revelation from Jesus that he gave to the New Testament church, Jesus' closest disciple—John, the "Beloved One"—told of a day that was soon to come when all of mankind would worship and honor the Lord. He wrote:

> *After this I looked, and there before me was a door standing open in heaven.* **— Revelation 4:1 (NIV)**

> *In the center, around the throne, were four living creatures, and they were covered with eyes, in front and in back.* — **Revelations 4:6 (NIV)**

> *Day and night they never stop saying: "Holy, holy, holy is the Lord God Almighty, who was, and is, and is to come."*
>
> *Whenever the living creatures give glory, honor and thanks to him who sits on the throne and who lives forever and ever, the twenty-four elders fall down before him who sits on the throne and worship him who lives for ever and ever. They lay their crowns before the throne and say:*
>
> *"You are worthy, our Lord and God, to receive glory and honor and power, for you created all things, and by your will they were created and have their being."* —**Revelation 4: 8–11 (NIV)**

What Does a True Worshipper Look Like?

As I mentioned previously, I have experienced many different styles of worship in many different countries across this planet. Worship styles and behaviors can vary greatly from culture to culture and church to church. In the book of Revelation, the apostle John told of visions about worship that showed what true worshipers really looked like.

John's worship in heaven began by recognizing four living creatures and twenty-four elders who had fallen down in worship before the Lamb. After hearing the voices of angels, John gazed heavenward and saw tens of thousands of angelic hosts, all praising God by saying, "Worthy is the Lamb." The words that John heard were simple but strong: "To him who sits on the throne and the Lamb be praise and honor and glory and power, for ever and ever!" John was overwhelmed by this expression of heartfelt worship.

According to John, true worshipers will "fall down before God." They will lay down their possessions at His feet and glorify His name.

That is how we, too, must learn to say, "Hallowed be Thy name." The first action we must take in growing a healthy prayer life is to acknowledge that our God is worthy to be praised and then do just that: worship Him with our true hearts. Before making any confessions, requests, or petitions, praising God must come first.

Join me in this prayer:

> Father, along with Jesus, Your Son, His disciples, and the many millions who have prayed this prayer since, I "hallow Your name" today. I thank You and praise You for all You have done in my life so far and for all that is yet to come. I praise You as Elohim, as Jehovah, as Adonai. El Shaddai and Immanuel, You are worthy of my worship, honor, and respect. Before I ask anything, confess anything, or pray anything else: I worship You. Amen.

WORKBOOK

Chapter 1 Questions

Question: Why did Jesus teach His disciples to start their prayers with worship? What happens if you neglect to honor God before making requests of Him? Where would this leave your relationship with God?

_____
_____
_____
_____
_____
_____
_____
_____
_____
_____
_____
_____
_____

Question: Many Bible verses, as well as the songs sung in church, describe the act of failing down before God in worship. Why do you think this physical reaction is linked to the presence of God?

Question: What do the names of God tell you about Him? Why do you think there are so many? What specific insights do you gain from some of the names given to Jesus (see Isaiah 9:6, for example)?

_____

_____

_____

_____

_____

_____

_____

Action: It's very easy to get into the habit of taking God for granted, yet He delights in spending time with us. To help break this habit, make a list of as many reasons for praising God as you can—not only for what He has done, but more importantly for who He is. Use your list to help you spend time in worship without asking Him for anything.

Chapter 1 Notes

CHAPTER TWO

Thy Kingdom Come: The Prayer Principle of Bringing God's Kingdom to the Earth

Your kingdom come, your will be done, on earth as it is in heaven. — **Matthew 6:10 (NIV)**

"All hail the king!"

When this cry went forth back in medieval times, it meant that the people who were gathered were about to be in the presence of royalty. It was a special event. It was a reason for them to present their very best self to the one who ruled over them, the one who wielded the greatest level of authority over their lives. It was an awe-inspiring event, one to be feared as well as anticipated.

We may not always acknowledge it, but when we come before God in prayer, we are entering the presence of the King—and not just any king, but the King of kings! It is a special event every time we sit at His feet.

When we pray as Jesus taught us to do, for "God's kingdom to come, on earth as it is in heaven," we are requesting that another, very special event will take place. We are asking that the rule of this King of kings will take place on the earth—that His power and His leadership will come to be seen as the ultimate authority in our world. We are recognizing Him as our true King, even over and above ourselves.

In 1 Chronicles 29:11–12, we read the following words about God's kingship:

> *Yours, LORD, is the greatness and the power and the glory and the majesty and the splendor, for everything in heaven and earth is yours. Yours, LORD, is the kingdom; you are exalted as head over all. Wealth and honor come from you; you are the ruler of all things. In your hands are strength and power to exalt and give strength to all.* **(NIV)**

One of the greatest kings who ever ruled in Bible times was described in the Old Testament as a "man after God's own heart": King David. And many of the Psalms attributed to this poet king record what he believed about God, his own King:

> *The LORD reigns forever; he has established his throne for judgment. He rules the world in righteousness and judges the peoples with equity.* — **Psalm 9:7–8 (NIV)**

> *The LORD sits enthroned over the flood; the LORD is enthroned as King forever.* — **Psalm 29:10**

Your throne, O God, will last for ever and ever; a scepter of justice will be the scepter of your kingdom. — **Psalm 45:6 (NIV)**

The LORD reigns, he is robed in majesty; the LORD is robed in majesty and armed with strength; indeed, the world is established, firm and secure. Your throne was established long ago; you are from all eternity. — **Psalm 93:1–2 (NIV)**

Ascribe to the LORD, all you families of nations, ascribe to the LORD glory and strength. Ascribe to the LORD the glory due his name; bring an offering and come into his courts. Worship the LORD in the splendor of his holiness; tremble before him, all the earth. Say among the nations, "The LORD reigns." — **Psalm 96:7–10a (NIV)**

As you can see, there was no doubt in the mind of King David, who had worshiped God since his own humble start as a shepherd boy, that God's kingdom was an essential foundation for every part of his life.

Don't Worry

Chaos, conflict, and wars throughout the world make it difficult to believe that God's kingdom has taken control on earth. It is for this reason Jesus taught us that we should pray for the kingdom of God to come on "earth as it is in heaven."

In the Psalms, King David declared, "The LORD has established his throne in heaven, and his *kingdom* rules over all" (Psalm 103:19 NIV, emphasis mine). In the

Lord's Prayer, Jesus taught us that we should seek the kingdom of God before we make any other request, including our need for personal provisions or care. The practice of praying the way Jesus teaches us to pray pushes aside the selfishness in our hearts and gets to the core of the matter: putting God and His will first, above every other thing in our lives.

Jesus urged His disciples to ask for God's presence and influence as their highest and greatest desire. This was to be the first request they made in their prayers, only following the acknowledgment of Him as the God of heaven, their source of provision, the "Hallowed One."

Thus, Jesus taught us that when we approach God, our prayers should not immediately jump into personal requests. Instead, we must come before our King with adoration of our heavenly Father and heartfelt worship of Him.

On one occasion, Jesus taught those who were listening to Him a basic principle of thinking about God's rule and God's kingdom before anything else. He explained that self-centered worry would destroy his listeners' belief in God's rule and counteract the results of their prayers. He said:

> *Therefore I tell you, do not worry about your life, what you will eat or drink; or about your body, what you will wear. Is not life more than food, and the body more than clothes?*
> *— Matthew 6:25 (NIV)*

When we engage in a prayer life that places God first, we are acknowledging who He is by honoring Him. We are asking for His influence to take control. We are setting our own desires, goals, and ambitions aside and allowing God to lead us in every aspect of our lives.

God's Rule Comes First

The teachings of Jesus were based on the rule of God in the hearts, minds, and lives of His listeners. One day, not long after John the Baptist was arrested, Jesus began His own ministry by proclaiming that the long-awaited kingdom of God had arrived:

> *After John was put in prison, Jesus went into Galilee, proclaiming the good news of God. "The time has come," he said. "The kingdom of God has come near. Repent and believe the good news!"* — **Mark 1:14–15 (NIV)**

The Gospel of Luke recorded that the driving force behind Jesus' earthly ministry was to first promote the kingdom of God. As Jesus told His followers, "I must proclaim the good news of the kingdom of God to the other towns also, because that is why I was sent" (Luke 4:43).

Long before Jesus ever taught about God's kingdom or His soon-to-be-established rule in the earth, King David wrote about this concept in many of the Psalms. And let's face it: King David knew how to define a kingdom! He had this to say about what God's kingdom was intended to be:

> ...dominion belongs to the LORD and He rules over the nations. — **Psalm 22:28 (NIV)**

> The LORD has established his throne in heaven, and his kingdom rules over all. — **Psalm 103:19 (NIV)**

> They tell of the glory of your kingdom and speak of your might. — **Psalm 145:11 (NIV)**

These passages of Scripture declare that God's kingdom is real, and as a result, the acknowledgment of this rule and reign should begin our every prayer. When a Christian prays a truly "healthy" prayer, he or she asks for God's authority and strength to be exerted above everything else—before any of his or her own needs, wants, or desires are considered.

God's Unique Kingdom

The apostle Paul was convinced that when God's kingdom takes first place, something unique is created. A light that will dispel the kingdom of darkness and bring forth the answers to our prayers begins to shine in our lives. As Paul wrote to the Colossian church, "He has rescued us from the dominion of darkness and brought us into the kingdom of the Son he loves…" (Colossians 1:13 NIV).

Paul believed that when we pray for God's kingdom to come on earth, we are asking for the radiance and strength of God's Son to lead the way, to come first in our world, and to take control before we ever even consider our own needs and requests. And to keep us from an unhealthy degree of selfishness, this type of prayer places God firmly in His role as King and opens our eyes to our position of servitude. This redirects us away from our tendency toward self-centeredness and reorients us to the will of God.

The Will of God

Jesus told the early believers that as they prayed for God's kingdom to come to the earth, they should also request that His will would be fulfilled, with the words "Thy will be done." In his letter to the Roman church, the apostle Paul said, "Do not conform to the pattern of this world, but be transformed by the renewing of your mind. Then you will be able to test and approve what God's will is—his good, pleasing and perfect will" (Romans 12:2 NIV).

Jesus taught that obeying God creates a unique relationship between ourselves and our Father. On one occasion, Jesus even said, "Whoever does God's will is my brother and sister and mother" (Mark 3:35 NIV). Yet, how are we ever able to really know the will of God?

It will come to us, springing forth from our longing for God's kingdom to be manifested on the earth. The *will of God* and the *kingdom of God* cannot be separated. When we pray for God's will to be done, we are referring to an action we would have take place—an event that would allow the rule of God to become dominant in a certain matter or area. God's authority must take precedence over any personal view that we might have. Jesus made this clear when He said these words:

> Not everyone who says to me, "Lord, Lord," will enter the kingdom of heaven, but only the one who does the will of my Father who is in heaven. Many will say to me on that day, "Lord, Lord, did we not prophesy in your name and in your name drive out demons and in your name perform many miracles?" Then I will tell them plainly, "I never knew you. Away from me, you evildoers!" — **Matthew 7:21–23 (NIV)**

For true believers to be obedient to the Lord, they must be faithful to following His guidance. When Jesus taught His disciples to pray for the will of God to take place on earth, He was calling for them to recognize God's plan and design as superior to anything man might come up with. In this way, Jesus taught us that when we pray, we are to acknowledge God as the Creator and the sovereign King of the universe. As Peter Gentry and Stephen Wellum write in *Kingdom Through Covenant*, "From the opening verses of Genesis, God is introduced and identified as the all-powerful Lord who created the universe by His word, while He Himself is uncreated, independent, self-existent, self-sufficient, and in need of nothing outside himself."[7]

Let's pray.

Heavenly Father, I worship You. Hallowed be Your name. I desire to see Your kingdom come on this earth—and not just in the realm of politics or world affairs, but in my own world as well. I long for Your wishes and Your will to come to pass, even before I want my own needs and desires to be met. Make this earthly world a heavenly place through Your presence and Your plan, and let it begin in my life. Amen.

WORKBOOK

Chapter 2 Questions

Question: When you pray for God's will to be done, what are you saying? Where does that leave your own personal wishes and desires?

_____

_____

_____

_____

_____

_____

_____

_____

_____

_____

Question: How did Jesus illustrate this principle in His own life? Do you think it was always an easy decision for Him? What did it cost Him?

_____
_____
_____
_____
_____
_____
_____
_____
_____
_____
_____
_____
_____
_____
_____
_____
_____
_____
_____

Question: Why do you think God described David as "a man after my own heart?" How did David's life experiences, both before and after he became king, influence his sense of God's kingdom?

Action: Take a few minutes to consider areas of your life where you struggle to say, "Your will be done." Pray that God will show you where you need to submit to His ruling and ask Him for the strength to be able to put His kingdom first.

Chapter 2 Notes

CHAPTER THREE

Give Us This Day: The Prayer Principle of Trusting in God's Provision

Give us today our daily bread. — **Matthew 6:11 (NIV)**

Do you *truly* and *honestly* believe that God will provide and take care of those He loves? Is it possible to receive the supplies that you need for daily life—needs like milk, bread, and clothing—from the God of all creation?

Jesus taught His disciples to call on their heavenly Father for their daily provisions. Many theologians and scholars believe that the phrase "Give us this day our daily bread" is better translated as "Give us our food for today."

By asking for our needs to be met in this way, we are acknowledging that God is the Provider of everything we already have and everything we will ever need. It is a mistake to think that we are the providers for ourselves or that we are even capable of such a task. On the contrary, Jesus taught His disciples to trust God daily.

Recognizing God as the Creator

There are many people who do not recognize God as the Creator of everything that exists, so the idea of acknowledging Him as the One who provides for all of their needs makes no sense to them. However, those who do see God's true nature and character as the designer and sustainer of the universe have little problem in recognizing Him as the Creator of everything with which they have been blessed. The prophet Nehemiah understood this:

> You alone are the LORD. You made the heavens, even the highest heavens, and all their starry host, the earth and all that is on it, the seas and all that is in them. You give life to everything, and the multitudes of heaven worship you. — **Nehemiah 9:6 (NIV)**

Nehemiah recognized that God was the Creator of all. We would do well to make our requests known to the One who gives life to everything.

Recognizing God as the Owner of All

A healthy prayer life acknowledges the true nature and character of God. In His teaching on the Lord's Prayer, Jesus told His followers to ask for bread from their heavenly Father. By using this illustration, He was helping them to understand and recognize that their needs went far beyond the mere satisfaction of physical hunger.

When a cook takes flour and creates bread, the result is much more than food. Before a cook can use flour, a miller must grind the grain into flour. Before the mill can produce flour from grain, a seed must be planted in the ground to produce the wheat. A cook may be skilled in creating the bread, but it was God who produced the elements of the earth that grow and feed the seed before it ever even makes it to an oven. God is owner and creator of all things.[8]

> *You are worthy, our Lord and God, to receive glory and honor and power, for you created all things, and by your will they were created and have their being.* **— Revelation 4:11 (NIV)**

Recognizing God as Our Provider

When we pray the words "give us this day," we are recognizing God as the giver of all good things and we are acknowledging our trust in Him to provide those things for us. When we engage in this type of prayer, we are better able to recognize God's goodness. Humble prayer sets our minds on the generosity of our Creator and loving heavenly Father.

Jesus taught His disciples basic truths about God's love for people:

On one occasion Jesus told his followers not to worry about their life, what they would find to eat, or their physical body. He encouraged them to think of themselves as needing much more than food, physical well-being, and clothing.

Jesus pointed them toward the birds of the air and said, "They do not sow or reap, they have no storeroom or barn; yet God feeds them." (Luke 12:24 NIV) After sharing this vivid illustration, Jesus stated, "And how much more valuable you are than birds?" Therefore, He was telling them clearly, God's provisions are to be trusted.

After finishing my seminary work at Southeastern Baptist Theological Seminary in Wake Forest, North Carolina, I was called to serve at a new church in western North Carolina. As my wife and I came into the area, the first challenge on our hands was a major one. The church did not have a parsonage, and we did not have the financial resources needed to purchase a home. The year was 1986, and we had only $500 saved after spending everything else we had on three years of seminary tuition and then experiencing the birth of our first child.

The option of renting a place seemed best, so our family and our new church both began to pray that the Lord would provide for this very crucial need in our lives.

Several weeks before our move was to take place, we were introduced to a man who had a small house for sale. Even knowing the limitations that we were facing, I went to take a look at the property. As I stood in what I thought would make a perfect home for my wife, our new baby boy, and me, I also felt a sense of doubt. How could we ever move into this home?

During my first few minutes in discussion with the homeowner, he asked me why I was moving to town. I told him that I had just finished seminary and that I had been called to pastor a church outside of town. He began to smile. It turned out that he and his family were members of the Methodist church in town and their son had just left to start his own seminary studies!

He then asked me how much money I had to put down on the house. I was embarrassed to say, "All I have is five hundred dollars."

But without hesitation, the man said, "That is perfect. Do you think you can get the loan you need for the rest?"

Without hesitation, I replied, "I sure can!" I was young, and I had never bought a house before. How much trouble could it be to secure a loan for a home?

All I knew was that God had called me to this new church and that He had a plan for my family. Not only did my heavenly Father find us the perfect home in which to live, but He was already working on our behalf to help us be able to move in right when we needed to do so. In my new congregation was an elder who had already begun the process of helping secure us a home loan with my five hundred dollars.

My young family moved into our own house because the Lord, the Provider, was at work.

Can We Really Trust God to Provide for Our Needs?

Jesus told an interesting parable about how God provides for those He loves. This lesson is found in the Gospel of Luke.

> Then Jesus told His disciples a parable to show them that they should always pray and not give up. He said: "In a certain town there was a judge who neither feared God nor cared what people thought. And there was a widow in that town who kept coming to him with the plea, 'Grant me justice against my adversary.'
>
> "For some time he refused. But finally he said to himself, 'Even though I don't fear God or care what people think, yet because this widow keeps bothering me, I will see that she gets justice, so that she won't eventually come and attack me!'" — **Luke 18:1–5 (NIV)**

During the time when Christ walked on this earth, a widow would be classified as the most needy member of society. The woman in this story had no one to care for her or provide for her needs. She would have been considered the poorest of the poor.

Jesus revealed the chief quality of this woman: *persistence.* She was willing to call on the rich man for help over and over again. After days and days of her constant badgering, the judge finally gave in to her unceasing pleas.

After telling this story to those who were listening, Jesus then went on:

> *Listen to what the unjust judge says. And will not God bring about justice for his chosen ones, who cry out to Him day and night? Will He keep putting them off? I tell you, He will see that they get justice, and quickly. However, when the Son of Man comes, will He find faith on the earth?*
> *— Luke 18:6–8 (NIV)*

In this parable, Jesus was asking two simple questions:

- "…will God not bring about justice for His chosen ones, who cry out to Him?
- "…will He keep putting them off?"

Jesus answered these questions in the affirmative. God will see to it that all of those who call on His name are cared for. One of the most reassuring facts about God is that He knows our needs before we even ask for His provision.

> *So do not worry, saying, "What shall we eat?" or "What shall we drink?" or "What shall we wear?" For the pagans run after all these things, and your heavenly Father knows that you need them. — Matthew 6:31–32 (NIV)*

Before He made this promise, Jesus warned His disciples to pay close attention to where they placed their focus. We typically find ourselves in prayer about three basic issues: our needs, our desires, and our anxieties.[9] But the fact remains that our loving heavenly Father knows about *each* of these issues before we even know about them.

Prayer is all about trusting in our Father. We must seek to place greater trust in the God who created us and become less preoccupied with our own needs. This will demonstrate that we truly believe that our heavenly Father is a loving Provider.

However, we will never really appreciate God's provision for our needs, our desires, or our anxieties until we place Him in His proper position as King, giving Him the place of highest worship and reverence in our lives.

James wrote these words: "You do not have because you do not ask God" (James 4:2 NIV).

The process of seeking God's provision in our lives does not need to be selfish. This practice is an act that, when done correctly, maintains a clear understanding of our true relationship with God. Peter understood what a healthy connection with God looked like and he described it when he told the early church, "Cast all your anxiety on Him, because He cares for you." (1 Peter 5:7)

Pray with me:

> Dear heavenly Father, thank You for caring for all of my needs. Thank You that You know every issue that I have—whether it be a need, a desire, or an anxiety—before I am even aware of it, let alone ask for Your help. You are so good to me! I praise and worship You, I see Your will in my life, and I thank You for Your great provision for me. Amen.

WORKBOOK

Chapter 3 Questions

Question: How much do you trust in God's provision? Do you truly believe He is able and willing to supply all your needs, or are you trying desperately to do that for yourself?

_____
_____
_____
_____
_____
_____
_____
_____
_____
_____

Question: In the passage in Luke 12, Jesus refers to God's care for all His creation, including birds and wildflowers. What insight does this give you regarding His love for you? How would it change your life if you could stop worrying about the future?

_____
_____
_____
_____
_____
_____
_____
_____
_____
_____

Question: What does it mean to "seek first kingdom of God"? How does that affect your outlook, values, and priorities?

_____
_____
_____
_____
_____

_____

_____

_____

_____

_____

_____

_____

Action: Most of our prayers focus on our needs, desires, and anxieties, yet God has promised to take care of everything. Write down these three headings and add a Scripture to memorize regarding God's provision in each of these areas. Ask Him to help you see where you are afraid and failing to trust in His love for you.

Chapter 3 Notes

CHAPTER FOUR

Forgive Us Our Trespasses: The Prayer Principle of Seeking God's Forgiveness

Forgive us our debts, as we also have forgiven our debtors.
— *Matthew 6:12 (NIV)*

Are you ready for a challenge?

Until this part of the Lord's Prayer, Jesus had essentially asked His followers to worship the Father, putting His Kingdom goals and purposes first in their lives before they ask for their needs, desires, and anxieties to be addressed. But this request of the Lord as part of the prayer He is teaching us to pray—*this* is a challenge. Believing and accepting God's forgiveness *requires* something of me—some kind of action, at some kind of cost.

If I want to be forgiven, I myself must be willing to forgive. Does God actually require me to forgive someone else if I wish to be forgiven? Yes! He really, truly does. The Bible gives us very clear instructions about this subject of forgiveness.

When forgiveness is mentioned in the Old Testament, the Bible generally is speaking of the removal of any barriers that separate us from the presence of God, like when the prophet Isaiah wrote, "I ... am he who blots out your transgressions, for my own sake, and remembers your sin no more." (Isaiah 43:25 NIV). When we are forgiven by God, it takes a mighty act of His grace and mercy to mend the relationship that was broken.

When it comes to the subject of forgiveness, Jesus teaches that in order to receive it, we have to be willing to give it away to others who offend us. Christians cannot receive the heavenly Father's forgiveness for their own sinful actions unless they are willing to forgive those who have offended them or harmed them in some way.

If we hold on to the offenses of others, it will stifle our own experience of forgiveness from God. Dr. Chuck Lawless observes of the influence of an unforgiving heart, "Hanging on to bitterness, we experience both the continued pain and anguish of knowing that God is not pleased with our attitude."[10]

Forgiving someone for his or her past actions is not an easy task. Such hurts carry with them a wealth of emotions, often fueled by bitterness. The action of forgiveness calls for a person to take on a mature attitude, giving up his or her own justifications to hate or be angry with someone for real, possibly very painful harm or injury.

But forgiveness is never determined by another's behavior, only by our own. Jesus told His disciples that forgiveness must be fueled by our attitude and our personal actions.

> *You have heard that it was said, 'Eye for eye, and tooth for tooth.' But I tell you, do not resist an evil person. If anyone slaps you on the right cheek, turn to them the other cheek also. And if anyone wants to sue you and take your shirt, hand over your coat as well.* — **Matthew 5:38–40 (NIV)**

This type of behavior is counterintuitive and very difficult to put into practice. Most people will find this impossible to do without a nature that is stronger than their own, a nature that is supernaturally infused into them.

Forgiveness Is a Sign of Maturity

When Jesus called His disciples to take this type of action in their prayer lives, He was showing them that the action of forgiving another person is one of the highest, most expressive forms of healthy spiritual behavior. In other words, forgiveness can only be practiced by those who have come to understand what it means to truly be forgiven themselves.

A true sign that an individual has been born again can be seen when he or she is able to follow the forgiving Spirit of Jesus and practice this unconditional way of forgiving. As our divine example, Jesus hung on the cross during one of the most brutal and savage executions known to mankind, yet He was heard crying out, "Father, forgive them, for they do not know what they are doing" (Luke 23:34 NIV).

The forgiving action of a follower of this forgiving Christ is a behavior that is unique in our world of self-centeredness and me-first attitudes. It warms the heart and cools the temper.

Forgiveness Is a Requirement

Those who forgive in this way understand that their attitudes and decisions to forgive can never change past actions, but forgiveness does open up the path toward a positive future. As Jesus taught His disciples, "If you forgive other people when they sin against you, your heavenly Father will also forgive you. But if you do not forgive others their sins, your Father will not forgive your sins." (Matthew 6:14–15 NIV).

If we are unwilling to forgive the actions of someone else, this will create unhealthy resentment. And ironically, this type of behavior does not affect the one it is aimed toward; it consumes the mind and heart of the one refusing to forgive! When Simon Peter asked Jesus about this subject, He explained forgiveness further to Peter and the rest of His disciples:

> *Then Peter came to Jesus and asked, "Lord, how many times shall I forgive my brother or sister who sins against me? Up to seven times?"*
>
> *Jesus answered, "I tell you, not seven times, but seventy-seven times."* — **Matthew 18:21–22 (NIV)**

This behavior does not refer to a set number of occasions that should be taken into account for forgiveness. In fact, this phrase "seventy-times seven" indicated, in the culture of Jesus' day, an infinite number of times—which in the case of forgiveness can only be brought about by an attitude of love and graciousness that is fueled by the Holy Spirit, not the spirit of man.

When we think of forgiveness at its best and at its worst, a certain parable of Jesus in Matthew 18 may come to mind:

A king wanted to settle up his accounts with his servants. Just as he was doing so, a man who owed the king ten thousand bags of gold was brought to him. Because this man was not able to pay his debt, the master ordered that he and his entire family and every possession he had should be sold to repay the debt.

The distraught servant fell on his knees before the king, begging for patience. Fortunately for the servant, his master took pity on him, canceled the debt, and let him and his family go free.

In the very next scene, when the servant left his master's place, he spotted a fellow servant who owed *him* a much smaller debt than he'd just had erased. Rather than practice the forgiveness he had just experienced, the man grabbed his fellow servant and began to choke him, demanding immediate payment.

Despite the second servant's pleas, the first man would not show mercy. He had his fellow servant thrown into prison until the debt was paid. But when the other servants saw what had happened, they were outraged.

They went and told their master everything that had happened.

The master called the first servant in and immediately reinstated the original debt. The unforgiving man was himself declared unforgiven. In anger, his master handed him over to the jailers to be tortured until his entire debt was repaid. According to Jesus, the moral of the story is this: "This is how my heavenly Father will treat each of you unless you forgive your brother or sister from your heart" (Matthew 18:35 NIV).

Jesus showed His disciples that the act of forgiveness would cause their spiritual lives to grow exponentially. And this is true for the modern believer, too. An unwillingness to forgive is self-defeating, but forgiving others freely is a virtue to be sought after and cultivated.

Am I Willing to Forgive Others?

Has anyone ever offended you to the point that you became extremely angry? Forgiveness is not always easy! In fact, if an offense was bad enough to require forgiveness, then by definition, that forgiveness is hard to offer.

Forgiveness between you and God may frequently be "expected," but what about forgiveness between you and another person? This is especially hard if that person is the one who has hurt you the most in your life.

Forgiveness is a choice. It is not something that anyone can make you do. Forgiveness also has a qualifying action that accompanies it. Jesus explained this interplay between attitude and action when He spoke these words to His disciples:

> For if you forgive other people when they sin against you, your heavenly Father will also forgive you. But if you do not forgive others their sins, your Father will not forgive your sins. — **Matthew 6:14–15 (NIV)**

Jesus also taught His disciples about forgiving others when He said:

> If your brother or sister sins against you, rebuke them; and if they repent, forgive them. Even if they sin against you seven times in a day and seven times come back to you saying, "I repent," you must forgive them. — **Luke 17:3–4 (NIV)**

As Jesus taught His disciples, He also challenged them to think about how prolonged resentment bred anxiety and depression in their hearts. Freeing yourself from the bondage of resentment and hatred is a challenge. Pent-up anger will drain you in every area: physically, mentally, and spiritually.

People who carry an unforgiving attitude throughout their lives will produce bitterness in their souls, and this fueled bitterness will create even further grudges that will wound the heart and mind. It is a destructive cycle, and for the health of our hearts it should be stopped as soon as it is recognized.

As Paul exhorted in his letter to the Ephesians:

> *Do not let any unwholesome talk come out of your mouths, but only what is helpful for building others up according to their needs, that it may benefit those who listen. And do not grieve the Holy Spirit of God, with whom you were sealed for the day of redemption. Get rid of all bitterness, rage and anger, brawling and slander, along with every form of malice. Be kind and compassionate to one another, forgiving each other, just as in Christ God forgave you.*
> — ***Ephesians 4:29–32 (NIV)***

Jesus has made it clear that forgiveness from God and forgiveness of others cannot be separated. But thank God—He is not keeping a scoreboard, nor does He follow a merit-based system that allows us to earn favor with Him. Instead, our decision to forgive those others who have wronged us bears a strong witness to the fact that we know we have been forgiven by Him.

Let's pray together.

> Heavenly Father, You do not ask something easy of me when You ask me to forgive! But I know how much You have forgiven me in my own life, and I make the choice to extend that mercy, that grace, that forgiveness to those who need the same thing from me. In that way, I can demonstrate Your amazing grace and love to a world desperate to know You. Amen.

WORKBOOK

Chapter 4 Questions

Question: Have you ever been generously forgiven by someone? Or have you ever had your apology rejected with no forgiveness? In each case, how did it make you feel?

_____
_____
_____
_____
_____
_____
_____
_____
_____
_____
_____

Question: Why is it so hard to forgive? What are some of the reasons why you are sometimes reluctant to give up a sense of grievance and anger?

_____

_____

_____

_____

_____

_____

_____

_____

_____

Question: When you refuse to forgive someone, who is most affected by your attitude? Why is forgiveness a choice, not an emotion? Which demonstrates more strength—to forgive or to refuse forgiveness—and why?

_____

_____

_____

_____

_____

_____

_____

_____

_____

_____

_____

Action: We often hear the expression "forgive and forget," but forgetting a bad experience or a hurtful remark is not the same as forgiving it. Ask God to shine His light into your heart and show you what is lurking in the shadows. Where do you need to offer forgiveness and resolve a painful memory?

Chapter 4 Notes

CHAPTER FIVE

Lead Us Not into Temptation: The Prayer Principle of Relying on God's Protection

Lead us not into temptation, but deliver us from evil one.
— **Matthew 6:14 (NIV)**

"Lead us not into temptation." What? What in the world did Jesus mean when He prayed *that*?

Does God ever "lead His children into temptation"? This phrase seems to contradict everything that Jesus had been teaching His disciples about the nature of our heavenly Father. How could it be that God would even consider an action that might cause His children to be tempted in any way? Doesn't this go against the very character of God?

Perhaps considering the real meaning of "temptation" in the original language of the Bible would help our understanding and clear up the confusion.

The Greek noun for *temptation* literally means "trial" or "test"[11] and the Greek verb for *to tempt* similarly means "to try" or "to test."[12] When the word *temptation* is used today in the English language, it most often refers to negative or evil behavior. However, this same Greek word is actually a *neutral* action word; it simply refers to a test, or a performance. In the New Testament, it frequently focuses on testing the character or qualities of an individual, such as in Matthew 4:1, when we read that "Jesus was led by the Spirit into the wilderness to be *tempted* by the devil" (NIV, emphasis mine).

Jesus' teachings about temptation were twofold. The first understanding He shared is that we must recognize that God has the ability to protect us from times of trials or testing. However, Jesus' second point was that when temptations do come into our lives, God has the strength ready and available for us to overpower them.

Inner Temptation

What causes sin to be generated from within ourselves? The fact is, sin is fueled by a temptation that, simply put, comes from a sinful heart. Many religions and cults do not believe in original sin. They argue that the idea that someone is born into the world already possessing a sinful nature could not possibly make sense, but anyone who has heard a toddler yell "no!" or "mine!" understands that original sin is all too real.

To avoid this reality, people try to define *inner temptation* in many other ways. But here are some basic facts about inner temptation:

- God will never invite us to sin.
- Satan cannot force us to sin.
- When we fall into temptation, we have chosen wrongly.

Many people feel that inner temptation cannot be overcome. Even the apostle Paul, as spiritually "strong" as he was, spoke of the allure of inner sins. He wrote these words to the church at Rome:

> *I do not understand what I do. For what I want to do I do not do, but what I hate I do. And if I do what I do not want to do, I agree that the law is good. As it is, it is no longer I myself who do it, but it is sin living in me. For I know that good itself does not dwell in me, that is, in my sinful nature. For I have the desire to do what is good, but I cannot carry it out. For I do not do the good I want to do, but the evil I do not want to do—this I keep on doing. Now if I do what I do not want to do, it is no longer I who do it, but it is sin living in me that does it.* **— Romans 7:15–20 (NIV)**

When dealing with inner temptations, Christians don't have to rely on their own strength alone to help them overcome and succeed. Christians have the Holy Spirit and the power of God to call upon.

And according to Jesus, God's plan is never to leave His children to deal with spiritual temptation on their own. When Jesus was talking to His disciples about the future, He told them, "And I will ask the Father, and he will give you another advocate to help you and be with your forever…" (John 14:26 NIV).

As Christians, the Holy Spirit is continually working in our hearts to enable us, to encourage us, and to teach us how to choose wisely in every temptation we face.

Paul also believed that God would not allow any temptation to come our way that we could not endure. He wrote:

> No temptation has overtaken you except what is common to mankind. And God is faithful; he will not let you be tempted beyond what you can bear. But when you are tempted, he will also provide a way out so that you can endure it. — *1 Corinthians 10:13 (NIV)*

Outer Temptation

The story of Jesus' temptation in Matthew 4:1–11 reveals the power of all three types of outer temptations. For forty days and nights, Jesus wandered through the wilderness to prepare Himself for His soon-to-be-launched public ministry. Jesus' wilderness experience was to prepare Himself for what lay ahead.

During His time in the wilderness, however, the Bible says that Satan came to Jesus to present Him with three outer temptations. In the book of 1 John, Jesus' closest disciple categorized *outer temptation* in three distinct ways.

> For everything in the world—the lust of the flesh, the lust of the eyes, and the pride of life—comes not from the Father but from the world. —*1 John 2:16 (NIV)*

Outer temptation came at Jesus in the first forty days of His ministry. After His baptism, three types of sin, "the lust of the flesh, the lust of the eyes, and the pride of life," came at Him. Any outer temptation you face will also fall into one of these three categories.

The Lust of the Flesh

One of the greatest struggles human beings face when being tempted is the need to meet a physical desire, whether it be related to the lust of gluttony or to the seduction of sexual satisfaction.

The "lust of the flesh" was the temptation with which Satan approached Jesus first. Christ had already been in the wilderness for weeks, fasting to prepare Himself for His ministry. The enemy approached Jesus with the thing from which He was suffering most: physical hunger. After forty days of fasting, Jesus was starving. The desire to satisfy the needs of His earthly body was the first attack of the enemy.

The Old Testament tells a similar story of temptation about King David, who allowed his attraction to Bathsheba, the wife of his faithful officer Uriah, to lead to an adulterous affair. She became pregnant, and to cover up his sin, David called Uriah home from the battlefield and tried to encourage him to spend time with his wife. But when Uriah slept outside the king's palace instead, David had to create a new plan to cover his sin.

In the morning David wrote a letter to Joab [his commander in chief] and sent it with Uriah. In it he wrote, "Put Uriah out in front where the fighting is fiercest. Then withdraw from him so he will be struck down and die." — **2 Samuel 11:14–15 (NIV)**

The human body was created by God to experience various needs. Many of the pleasures we experience in life are derived from the godly fulfillment of these physical needs. However, when we allow these bodily needs to override our obedience to God, we fall into sin. The allure of the flesh is an outer temptation that can lead us away from the design and plan of God if we are not careful to avoid it. The lust of the flesh was what led David to commit adultery and to have one of his faithful generals killed on the battlefield. Our spiritual enemy, Satan, knows how to fuel the lust of the flesh, as he did with King David.

The Lust of the Eyes

In the second outer temptation, Satan showed Jesus the kingdoms of the world. He told Him that He could own them for Himself if He would only bow down and worship Satan (see Matthew 4:8–9). The lust of the eyes, in this case, was the appeal of wealth and power.

The eye is just one tool that our soul has been given to produce either goodness or evil in our lives. In illustrating the type of use of the eye, Jesus told His disciples:

Your eye is the lamp of your body. When your eyes are healthy, your whole body also is full of light. But when they are unhealthy, your body also is full of darkness. See to it, then, that the light within you is not darkness. Therefore, if your whole body is full of light, and no part of it dark, it will be just as full of light as when a lamp shines its light on you. — **Luke 11:34–36 (NIV)**

The Pride of Life

Satan tempted Jesus to show His importance by encouraging Him to test God. He took Jesus to a high pinnacle and told Him to throw himself down, but to call on God to save Him from the fall (Matthew 4:5–7). In this way, he reasoned, Jesus' ministry would be validated by a miraculous divine intervention.

This challenge was a temptation actually meant to test the Father, and it would have had Jesus asserting His importance above that of the heavenly Father. It was a temptation of extreme pride.

The writer of Proverbs has some strong words to say about pride:

> *When pride comes, then comes disgrace.* — **Proverbs 11: 2 (NIV)**

> *Pride goes before destruction, a haughty spirit before a fall.* — **Proverbs 16:18 (NIV)**

Pride is a strong tool in the hands of our spiritual enemy, and it can cause even devoted believers to fall into temptation. It can destroy the best of human beings, because it begins small but soon grows into massively destructive behavior that ruins entire lives.

These three tests of outer temptation (the lust of the flesh, the lust of the eyes, and the pride of life) essentially cover all types of sins, and Jesus was able to overcome each one of them in the desert. In his famous book on Christian apologetics, *Mere Christianity*, author and theologian C.S. Lewis shares some valuable insights about temptation in the life of Jesus. He writes:

> A silly idea is current that good people do not know what temptation means. This is an obvious lie. Only those who try to resist temptation know how strong it is. After all, you find out the strands of the German army by fighting against it, not by giving in. You find out the strength of a wind by trying to walk against it, not by lying down. A man who gives in to temptation after five minutes simply does not know what it would have been like an hour later. This is why bad people, in one sense, know very little about badness. They have lived a sheltered life but always giving in ... Christ, because He was the only man who never yielded to temptation, is also the only man who knows to the full what temptation means.

Spiritual Trials

God sometimes does allow trials to come our way. No one's life is ever completely free from problems and difficulties. After all, these give us the opportunity to grow. But Satan attempts to take these trials and distort them by turning them into temptations to sin.

Paul teaches us that God can make us strong through our trials:

> *But the Lord is faithful, and he will strengthen you and protect you from the evil one.* — ***2 Thessalonians 3:3 (NIV)***

Even the teachings of the Old Testament show how the Lord watches over His children during challenging times:

> *Be strong and courageous. Do not be afraid or terrified because of them, for the L*ord *your God goes with you; he will never leave you nor forsake you.* — ***Deuteronomy 31:6 (NIV)***

And Isaiah resounds these words found in Deuteronomy:

> *So do not fear, for I am with you; do not be dismayed, for I am your God. I will strengthen you and help you; I will uphold you with my righteous right hand.* — ***Isaiah 41:10 (NIV)***

A King's Words About God and Trials

King David was a man who endured many tests and trials. From slaying the giant Goliath as a child to being held accountable for his sinful behavior with Bathsheba, he had been through many ups and downs. Trials and temptations were a basic part of the teaching shared in the psalms of David:

But let all who take refuge in you be glad; let them ever sing for joy. Spread your protection over them, that those who love your name may rejoice in you. — **Psalm 5:11 (NIV)**

God is our refuge and strength, an ever-present help in trouble. — **Psalm 46:1 (NIV)**

Deliver me from my enemies, O God; be my fortress against those who are attacking me. — **Psalm 59:1 (NIV)**

Though I walk in the midst of trouble, you preserve my life. You stretch out your hand against the anger of my foes; with your right hand you save me. — **Psalm 138:7 (NIV)**

Keep me safe, Lord, from the hands of the wicked; protect me from the violent, who devise ways to trip my feet. — **Psalm 140:4 (NIV)**

Let's pray.

Heavenly Father, I face many temptations in this life—from many different sources—but You are my strong foundation throughout them all. Guide me. Teach me. And help me to stand strong in Your power. Amen.

WORKBOOK

Chapter 5 Questions

Question: *God does not lead His children into temptation. In your own words, what does this mean?*

Question: The things that tempt you to sin can come from within you or from your environment. Which type of temptation do you find most difficult to resist? How does God help you withstand temptations?

_____
_____
_____
_____
_____
_____
_____
_____
_____

Question: No one's life is free from difficulty and spiritual trials. What is the purpose of such trials? Why does God allow them, and what can we do to prepare for them?

_____
_____
_____
_____
_____

_____
_____
_____
_____
_____
_____
_____

Action: All temptation stems from three areas: the lust of the flesh, the lust of the eyes, and the pride of life. Using these headings, write down a list of the kind of things you struggle with, or have struggled with in the past. What practical steps can you take to overcome in these areas? Ask God to show you what you can do to help you stand firm against temptation.

Chapter 5 Notes

CHAPTER SIX

Thine Is the Kingdom, the Power, and the Glory: The Prayer Principle of Showcasing God's Kingdom, Power, and Glory

For Yours is the kingdom and the power and the glory forever. Amen. — **Matthew 6:13 (NASB)**

Your kingdom, Your power, and Your glory! What a combination! Do Christians today honestly want to surrender themselves over to this type of spiritual chemistry?

The teaching of the Lord's Prayer begins with acknowledging Jehovah as a Holy God to be honored and praised. As we come to the conclusion of Jesus' teaching about prayer, the disciples are taught to recognize His kingdom, His power, and His glory.

The Kingdom: True Prayer Starts and Ends Focused on God's Kingdom

What do we know about God's kingdom?

Jesus introduced the kingdom of God to humanity with a purpose. John's Gospel records these words of Christ: "'The time has come,' he said. 'The kingdom of God has come near. Repent and believe the good news!'" (Mark 1:15 NIV).

Jesus began His teaching by helping His disciples understand that true prayer has a Kingdom focus (Matthew 6:9–10). The Lord's Prayer starts by focusing on the Kingdom, and the closing of the prayer honors God and promotes His kingdom on earth.

How can God's kingdom take control of us as individuals and as congregations? It is not easy to surrender to the lordship of someone else, yet Jesus taught that for God's kingdom to take control, we must be willing to receive it with the faith of a small child.

He said, "Truly I tell you, anyone who will not receive the *kingdom of God* like a little child will never enter it" (Mark 10:15 NIV, emphasis mine). Jesus countered the ideas that to establish a kingdom, one must do it with force and strength. Instead, He said that to embrace the kingdom of God, Christ-followers should be humble, trusting, and simplistic—like children.

Until these traits are part of our lives, chances are we will miss God's kingdom and never understand it. Arrogance, pride, and self-sufficiency do not prepare us to be part of God's kingdom, but a faith that behaves like a child opens up all sorts of Kingdom understanding.

Those who are willing to give their lives to God receive a promise: Jesus assures those who seek the Kingdom that they will receive more information and wisdom from God. In the Gospel of Luke, Jesus is recorded as saying, "The knowledge of the secrets of the kingdom of God has been given to you, but to others I speak in parables, so that, 'though seeing, they may not see; though hearing, they may not understand'" (Luke 8:10 NIV).

Throughout the history of Christianity, those who have been used to spread the gospel and facilitate the growth of the church are those who have sought after God's kingdom as a trusting child.

A Dying Kingdom

The conversations of believers with their Lord and Creator are necessary if they wish to be part of God's kingdom. It is easy to become religious and allow a close relationship with God to disappear. Being involved in church work and events can be healthy and productive, but if those actions pull your attention away from the Father, they will push a life with God out of the picture.

It is easy to become so busy doing "God's work" that we do not have time for God and His kingdom. Busy work and a lot of talk is not always Kingdom work. This type of behavior brings up what Paul had to say about God's kingdom to the church at Corinth. He told the believers, "For the kingdom of God is not a matter of talk but of power" (1 Corinthians 4:20 NIV).

This is why a church without prayer—real, God-focused prayer—is a dead church.

The Power: True Prayer Ignites the Power of God

Often, church prayer meetings have become everything *but* a time for the power of God to be experienced. These events often become a time for Bible study or a mini-sermon from the pastor. By contrast, the New Testament book of Acts shows how the first-century believers came together to pray and experience the power of God. Their behavior was not complicated; it was fueled by the power of the Holy Spirit.

> *They all joined together constantly in prayer... — **Acts 1:14 (NIV)***
>
> *They devoted themselves to the apostles' teaching and to fellowship, to the breaking of bread and to prayer. — **Acts 2:42 (NIV)***
>
> *So Peter was kept in prison, but the church was earnestly praying to God for him. — **Acts 12:5 (NIV)***

The prayers of the believers sparked the moving of God within the early church. This type of prayer was an engagement with God that had an aim and a purpose. It was a time for Christians to place God in His proper place. True prayer in the early church gave God the praise He deserved.

God's Power Is Revealed in Many Ways

God's power was shown to the virgin Mary when the angel said, "The Holy Spirit will come on you, and the *power* of the Most High will overshadow you. So the holy one to be born will be called the Son of God" (Luke 1:35 NIV). The Creator's power was also revealed to the followers of John the Baptist when he told them, "I baptize you with water. But one who is more *powerful* than I will come, the straps of whose sandals I am not worthy to untie. He will baptize you with the Holy Spirit and fire" (Luke 3:16 NIV, emphasis mine).

On one occasion, those who were watching Jesus and His ministry made an observation about Him. The Gospel writer Luke recounts, "Jesus returned to Galilee in the *power* of the Spirit, and news about him spread through the whole countryside (Luke 4:14 NIV, emphasis mine). Luke also notes, "All the people were amazed and said to each other, 'What words these are! With authority and *power* he gives orders to impure spirits and they come out!'" (Luke 4:36 NIV, emphasis mine).

We Must Let Go of Our Power

One of the fundamental steps in dealing with God's influence over our lives is first to understand what destructive power is all about. Richard Foster explains personal power this way:

> What does the power that destroys look like? Think of Adam and Eve in the garden—given every pleasure, every

> delight, everything necessary for a good life. Yet they wanted more; they grasped and grabbed in a headlong rush to be like God, to know good and evil. The sin of the garden was the sin of power. They wanted to be more, to have more, to know more than is right. Not content to be creatures, they wanted to be gods.[13]

Adam and Eve proved from the beginning that depending on God and surrendering to His power is not easy. In fact, it is much easier for sinful men and women simply to ignore God and trust their own abilities than to be obedient servants of their Creator.

Insecurity in Trusting God's Power

Depending on God's power and not our own is a daily act of trust for the true Christian believer. Ed Stetzer and Thom Rainer declare that sincere prayer is a response to God's work and influence, rather than an activity intended to move Him into action.[14]

When Christian believers rely on God's power, their behavior connects with the Lord and their trust in Him produces results. These actions of praying believers who trust in God's power will help create praying churches that experience breakthroughs, see prayers answered, and commit to praying personally for each member and teaching all members how to live prayerful lives.

In the 1700s, William Williams, called the "Watts of Wales," wrote these words to the hymn "Guide Me, O Thou Great Jehovah":

Guide me, O my great Redeemer,

pilgrim through this barren land;

I am weak, but you are mighty;

hold me with your powerful hand.

True prayer recognizes the mighty power of God. When this takes place, it leads a believer to embrace the glory of God.

The Glory: True Prayer Glorifies God

There is a vast difference between those who practice prayer as a ritual and those who practice prayer as an act that praises God. Many people practice prayer as a habit. Some people only use prayer during occasions of perceived need or just before eating a meal. However, faithful Christians are those who pray constantly because they recognize a need to honor and praise God as a way of life.

For prayer to become more than a temporary, infrequent thing to do, some areas need attention to glorify God. True prayer must praise God (John 14:12–14), and sincere prayer must seek for God's kingdom and His will to prevail (1 John 5:14–15).

Glorifying God was witnessed at the beginning of the Gospel of Luke. Praising God was first done with perfection by the angels who appeared to the shepherds:

> *An angel of the Lord appeared to them, and the glory of the Lord shone around them, and they were terrified. But the angel said to them, "Do not be afraid. I bring you good news that will cause great joy for all the people. Today in the town of David a Savior has been born to you; he is the Messiah, the Lord."* — **Luke 2:9–11 (NIV)**

After the shepherds encountered the angels and became witnesses of the baby in a manger, they "returned, *glorifying* and praising God for all the things they had heard and seen" (Luke 2:20 NIV, emphasis mine). Glorifying God can become contagious, just as it did with the shepherds. It started with the angels and spread into the lives of the shepherds, who shared the Good News with others. Glorying God can spread like wildfire when fueled by the message of the Kingdom and its power.

The Apostle Paul also taught the early Christians how to give God glory. He told the first believers at Rome that many had fallen short of the "glory of God" (Romans 3:23 NIV). But he reminded them that the goal of every believer should be to recognize that all things come from Him and through Him and we should glorify Him forever (Romans 11:36). This is how he expressed a mindset of glorifying God:

> *Oh, the depth of the riches of the wisdom and knowledge of God! How unsearchable his judgments, and his paths beyond tracing out! "Who has known the mind of the Lord? Or who has been his counselor?" "Who has ever given to God, that God should repay them?" For from him and through him and for him are all things. To him be the **glory** forever! Amen.* — **Romans 11:33–36 (NIV, emphasis mine)**

When writing to young Timothy, Paul likewise demonstrated his practice of giving God the glory:

> Now to the King eternal, immortal, invisible, the only God, be honor and **glory** for ever and ever. Amen. — **1 Timothy 1:17 (NIV, emphasis mine)**

Prayer must acknowledge the Kingdom as belonging to God, the power of His majesty, and the glory of His name.

Prayer Is Essential!

Jesus' teaching about prayer is the solid foundation needed to grow spiritually. A healthy prayer life is a foretaste of heaven.

Whether you are building a personal life of prayer or a church prayer ministry, this basic fact remains clear: *prayer is essential!*

Only by humbling ourselves and seeking God through consistent, extended times of prayer with His Word in hand will we grow close to Him. And only through this kind of relationship will we be able to know and enjoy His presence and everything that comes with it.

WORKBOOK

Chapter 6 Questions

Question: In what ways do you deny God His rightful position in your life? If you were more keenly and consistently aware of His glory and power, how would your daily life change?

_____
_____
_____
_____
_____
_____
_____
_____
_____
_____
_____

Question: In Acts, the early church had a constant awareness of God's power and their dependence on Him. To what extent was that linked to both the persecution and the miracles they witnessed daily? To what extent do you think followers of Christ today have lost that awareness—and why?

_____
_____
_____
_____
_____
_____
_____
_____
_____
_____

Question: Why do so many church prayer meetings end up losing focus? Is public prayer more challenging than private prayer? What can be done to bring prayer back to the heart of the church?

_____
_____
_____
_____

_____

_____

_____

_____

_____

_____

_____

Action: Ask God to give you a heart to seek Him in prayer. Make a note in your journal of your church's next prayer meeting and join in prayer with others. If a prayer group seems to be lacking in your fellowship, consider whether God is calling you to start one yourself.

Chapter 6 Notes

REFERENCES

Notes

1. Spurgeon, Charles. *The Power in Prayer*. New Kensington, PA: Whitaker House, 1996, p. 9.
2. Meton, Thomas. *Contemplative Prayer*. Garden City, NY: Doubleday, 1969, p. 11.
3. Miller, Paul E. *A Praying Life*. Colorado Springs, CO: NavPress, 2009, p. 38–9.
4. Spurgeon, Charles. *The Power in Prayer*. New Kensington, PA: Whitaker House, 1996, p. 10.
5. Eims, Leroy. *Prayer: More than Words*. NavPress: Colorado Springs, CO, 1982, p.43.
6. Colson, Charles. *The Body*. Dallas, TX: Word Publishing, 1992, p. 337.
7. Gentry, Peter J. and Stephen J. Wellum. *Kingdom Through Covenant*. Wheaton, IL: Crossway, 2012, p. 592.
8. Bispham, Elizabeth Casey. *Short Lesson Talks on the Lord's Prayer and the Ten Commandments*. George W. Jacobs & Company, 1906, p. 36.

9. Beltz, Bob. *Becoming a Man of Prayer.* Colorado Springs, CO: NavPress, 1996, p. 11.
10. Lawless, Chuck. *Discipled Warriors.* Kregel Publications, 2002, p. 176.
11. "3986. peirasmos." From *Strong's Concordance. Bible Hub.* http://biblehub.com/greek/3986.htm.
12. "3985. peirazó." From *Strong's Concordance. Bible Hub.* http://biblehub.com/greek/3985.htm.
13. Foster, Richard. *Money, Sex, and Power.* Hodder & Stoughton Ltd., 2009.
14. Stetzer, Ed and Thom Rainer. *Transformational Church.* B&H Publishers, 2010, p. 127.

About the Author

Dale is a graduate of Gardner-Webb University, where he earned his Bachelor of Arts degree. He also is a graduate of Southeastern Baptist Theological Seminary, where he received his Master of Divinity degree.

In 1999 Dale began his study in a doctoral program at the Southern Baptist Theological Seminary in Louisville, Kentucky. His studies took place while Thom Rainer was the Dean of the Billy Graham School of Missions and Evangelism. He was a member in one of the first cohorts to graduate from SBTS with a doctoral degree in Church Growth Consulting. His studies at SBTS focused on team development.

The title of Dale's doctoral thesis was *A Consultant's Strategy for Team Development Within the Local Church.*

Dale is also the author of *The Jethro Ministry, A Biblical Strategy for Teamwork and The Servant-Leadership Style of Jesus.* At present Dale is serving as the Senior Pastor of Poplar Springs Baptist Church in Moore, SC.

About Sermon To Book

SermonToBook.com began with a simple belief: that sermons should be touching lives, *not* collecting dust. That's why we turn sermons into high-quality books that are accessible to people all over the globe.

Turning your sermon series into a book exposes more people to God's Word, better equips you for counseling, accelerates future sermon prep, adds credibility to your ministry, and even helps make ends meet during tight times.

John 21:25 tells us that the world itself couldn't contain the books that would be written about the work of Jesus Christ. Our mission is to try anyway. Because in heaven, there will no longer be a need for sermons or books. Our time is now.

If God so leads you, we'd love to work with you on your sermon or sermon series.

Visit www.sermontobook.com to learn more.